D1306672

AMAZING SUPER SIMPLE INVENTIONS

SUPER SIMPLE

TELEGRAPH
PROJECTS

INSPIRING & EDUCATIONAL
SCIENCE ACTIVITIES

ALEX KUSKOWSKI

Consulting Editor, Diane Craig, M.A./Reading Specialist

Super Sandcastle

An Imprint of Abdo Publishing
abdopublishing.com

Published by Abdo Publishing, a division of ABDO, PO Box 398166, Minneapolis, Minnesota 55439. Copyright © 2016 by Abdo Consulting Group, Inc. International copyrights reserved in all countries. No part of this book may be reproduced in any form without written permission from the publisher. Super SandCastle™ is a trademark and logo of Abdo Publishing.

Printed in the United States of America, North Mankato, Minnesota
062015
092015

THIS BOOK CONTAINS
RECYCLED MATERIALS

Editor: Liz Salzmann
Content Developer: Nancy Tuminelly
Cover and Interior Design and Production: Mighty Media, Inc.
Photo Credits: Library of Congress, Mighty Media, Inc., Shutterstock, Wikicommons

The following manufacturers/names appearing in this book are trademarks: 3M™ Scotch®, Alltrade®, CraftSmart®, Duracell®, Rayovac®, Stanley®

Library of Congress Cataloging-in-Publication Data

Kuskowski, Alex, author.
  Super simple telegraph projects : inspiring & educational science activities / Alex Kuskowski ; consulting editor, Diane Craig, M.A./reading specialist.
    pages cm. -- (Amazing super simple inventions)
  Audience: K to grade 4
  ISBN 978-1-62403-732-0
1. Morse, Samuel Finley Breese, 1791-1872--Juvenile literature. 2. Morse code--Juvenile literature. 3. Telegraph--Experiments--Juvenile literature. 4. Telegraph--History--Juvenile literature. 5. Inventions--Juvenile literature. I. Title.
  TK5243.M7K87 2016
  621.383--dc23
                        2014049933

Super SandCastle™ books are created by a team of professional educators, reading specialists, and content developers around five essential components—phonemic awareness, phonics, vocabulary, text comprehension, and fluency—to assist young readers as they develop reading skills and strategies and increase their general knowledge. All books are written, reviewed, and leveled for guided reading and early reading intervention programs for use in shared, guided, and independent reading and writing activities to support a balanced approach to literacy instruction.

To Adult Helpers

The projects in this title are fun and simple. There are just a few things to remember to keep kids safe. Some projects require the use of sharp objects. Also, kids may be using messy materials such as paint. Make sure they protect their clothes and work surfaces. Review the projects before starting, and be ready to assist when necessary.

....

KEY SYMBOLS

Watch for these warning symbols in this book. Here is what they mean.

SHARP!
You will be working with a sharp object. Get help!

CONTENTS

TELEGRAPHS

AN INTRODUCTION

What came before telephones and computers? How did people send fast messages? They used the telegraph. It used electricity. It sent messages many miles in a few seconds!

Samuel Morse was a telegraph **innovator**. Find out what he did. Learn how the telegraph works. Discover it for yourself!

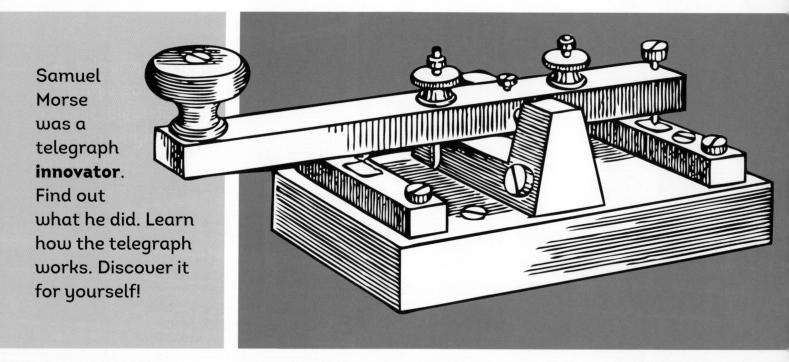

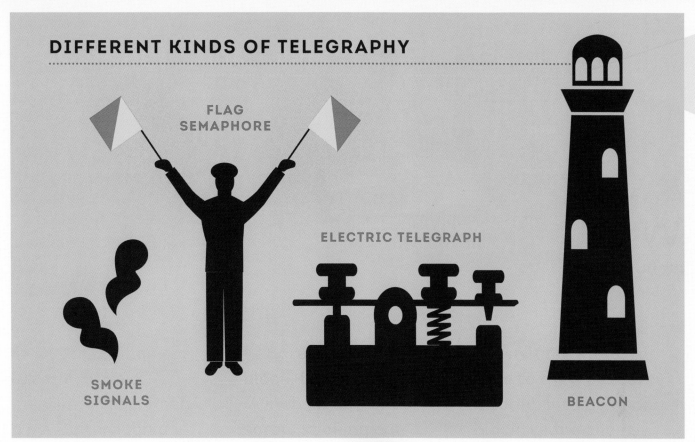

DIFFERENT KINDS OF TELEGRAPHY

FLAG SEMAPHORE

SMOKE SIGNALS

ELECTRIC TELEGRAPH

BEACON

Telegraphy means *distance writing*. Most kinds require the receiver to be within sight. The electric telegraph changed that!

SAMUEL MORSE

Samuel Morse got a patent for the telegraph. He made up a code.

He used the code to send telegraph messages. He called it Morse code.

Morse's telegraph could send a message fast. The sender gave the message to a telegraph **operator**.

OTHER IMPORTANT PEOPLE

William Sturgeon. He invented the electromagnet. It sent signals through wires.

Harrison Dyar. He recorded electrical sparks on paper. It was the first telegram.

The **operator** changed the message into Morse code. The code used short and long sounds.

Another operator listened at the other end. The operator wrote down the message. It was called a telegram.

THEN TO NOW

A TIMELINE OF THE TELEGRAPH

The semaphore line was built in France. It had towers with arms. The arms could move. Later, people used flags.

William Sturgeon invented the electromagnet. It could send electricity through a wire.

Joseph Henry invented the electric **relay**. It could pass signals from one wire to another.

1792   **1809**   **1824**   **1826**   **1835**

Samuel Thomas von Sömmering made a telegraph. It had 35 wires. It sent a message 2.2 miles (3.5 km).

Harrison Dyar sent the first telegraph message in the United States. It used one wire. The wire made sparks. The sparks made marks on paper.

MORSE CODE

People still use Morse code. It can be used when phones don't work. Some people learn Morse code for their jobs. Even space **shuttles** have telegraphs on board! They use them in **emergencies**.

The US government began using Morse's telegraph. The first line went between Washington, DC, and Baltimore.

The telephone was invented! It became an important way to pass **information**.

The teleprinter was invented. It had a keyboard. **Operators** didn't need to know Morse code.

1838 **1844** **1866** **1876** **1880**

Samuel Morse showed people his telegraph in New Jersey.

A telegraph wire went across the Atlantic Ocean. People could send messages across the ocean in seconds.

BE AN INVENTOR

LEARN HOW TO THINK LIKE AN INVENTOR!

Inventors have a special way of working. It is a series of steps called the Scientific Method. Follow the steps to work like an inventor.

THE SCIENTIFIC METHOD

1. QUESTION

What question are you trying to answer? Write down the question.

2. GUESS

Try to guess the answer to your question. Write down your guess.

3. EXPERIMENT

Think of a way to find the answer. Write down the steps.

KEEP TRACK

There's another way to be just like an inventor. Inventors make notes about everything they do. So get a notebook. When you do an experiment, write down what happens in each step. It's super simple!

4. MATERIALS

What supplies will you need? Make a list.

5. ANALYSIS

Do the experiment. What happened? Write down the results.

6. CONCLUSION

Was your guess correct? Why or why not?

MATERIALS

-inch (2 cm) screws

acrylic paint

clear tape

coated copper wire

D batteries

electrical tape

flashlight

foam paintbrush

iron nails

metal tab tape

notepad

pencil

Here are some of the materials that you will need.

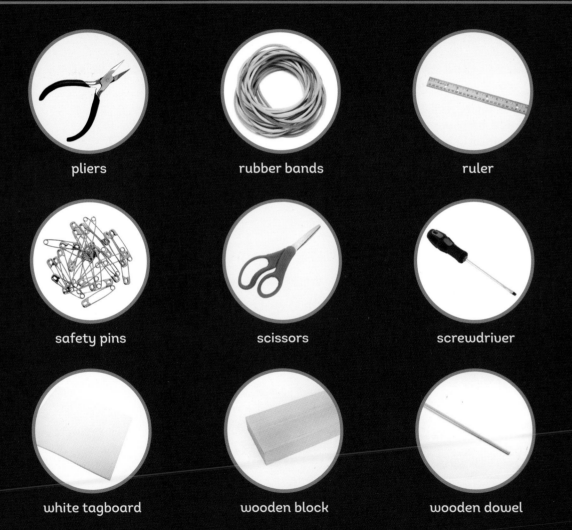

pliers

rubber bands

ruler

safety pins

scissors

screwdriver

white tagboard

wooden block

wooden dowel

SEMAPHORE FLAGS

Send a secret message!

MATERIALS: white tagboard, ruler, scissors, pencil, newspaper, acrylic paint, foam paintbrush, 4 24-inch (61 cm) wooden dowels, clear tape

Semaphore flags are used to pass **information**. Learn how to make your own flags.

HOW DOES IT WORK?

Flag semaphore is a way to pass information long distance. People use the flags to spell words. Find the alphabet on page 17. Send messages to your friends!

MAKE SEMAPHORE FLAGS

① Cut a 10-inch (25 cm) square out of tagboard.

② Draw a line from the bottom left corner to the top right corner. Turn the square over. Draw a line between the same corners.

③ Cover your work surface with newspaper. Paint the bottom triangle yellow. Paint the top triangle red. Let the paint dry. Turn the square over. Paint the triangles on the other side the same way. Let the paint dry.

④ Lay a dowel along one edge of the flag. Make sure the red triangle is on top. Tape the dowel to the flag.

⑤ Repeat steps 1 through 4 to make three more flags. Make two blue and white flags to use on land.

FLAG ALPHABET

Learn the semaphore code!

People use semaphore signals to send messages. Try it with your friends. Make the semaphore flags on pages 14 and 15. Then stand far away from each other. Use the code to pass secret messages.

You don't need flags to send semaphore messages. You can use just your arms. But the flags make the signals easier to see.

Flags used at sea are red and yellow. Flags used on land are white and blue.

SEMAPHORE ALPHABET

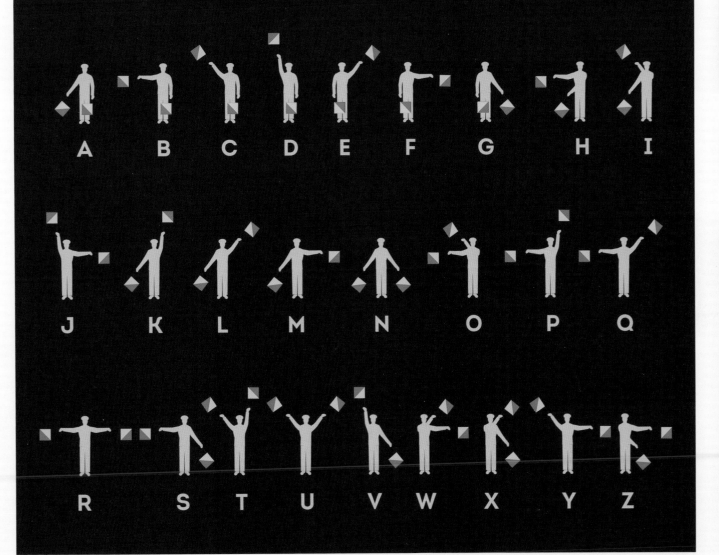

ELECTRIC MAGNET

Make the magnet that changed the world!

MATERIALS: coated copper wire, pliers, scissors, ruler, iron nail, D battery, electrical tape, safety pins

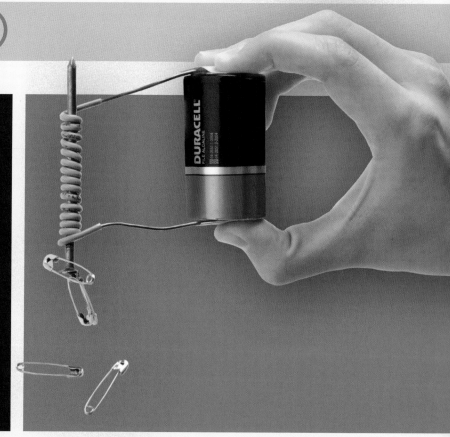

This magnet made the telegraph possible! It can pass electricity through wires.

HOW DOES IT WORK?

The wire and **battery** make a circuit. The circuit makes electricity. Electricity turns the nail into a magnet. The safety pins stick to the metal.

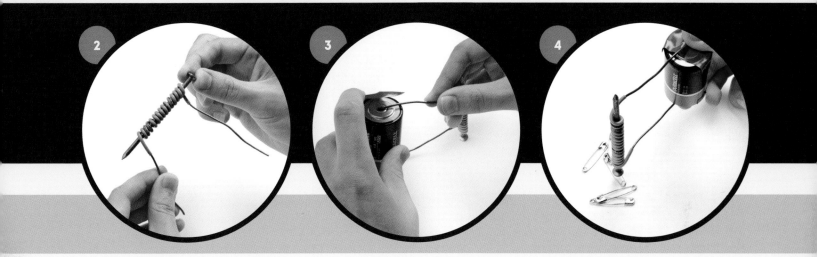

MAKE AN ELECTRIC MAGNET

① Cut a piece of wire 15 inches (38 cm) long. Strip 2 inches (5 cm) of coating off each end.

② Wrap the coated part of the wire around the nail.

③ Put each end of the wire on one end of the **battery**. Tape them in place.

④ Hold the nail over the safety pins.

How to Strip Wire

Use the scissors to cut through the coating. Cut all around the wire. Be careful not to cut the wire. Then pull the coating off with pliers.

TELEGRAPH

Make your own electric telegraph!

MATERIALS: metal tab tape, ruler, scissors, 7 ¾ inch (2 cm) screws, screwdriver, 3 × 2-inch (7.5 x 5 cm) wooden block, 13 × 3-inch (33 × 7.5 cm) wooden block, 2 D batteries, rubber band, iron nail, hammer, coated copper wire, pliers

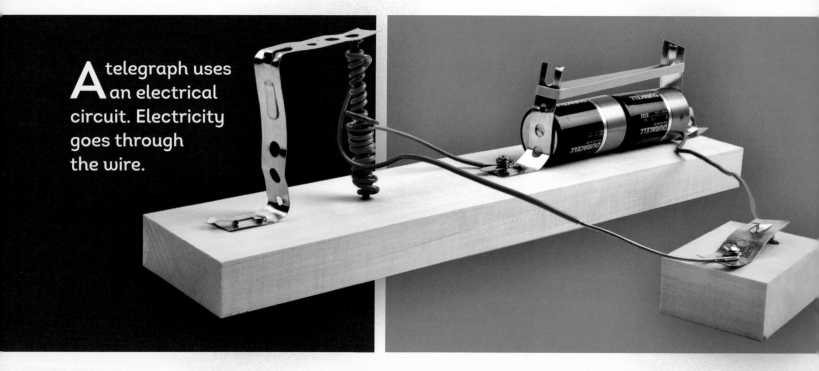

A telegraph uses an electrical circuit. Electricity goes through the wire.

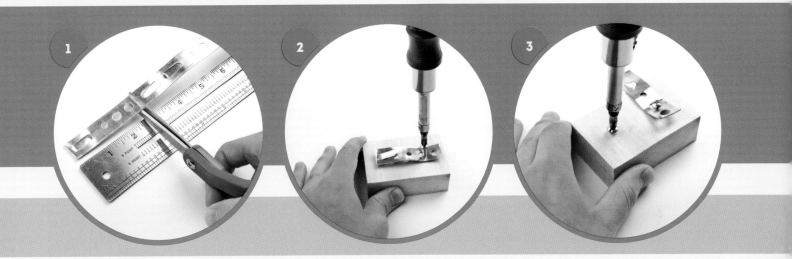

MAKE THE SENDER

1 Cut a 2.5-inch (6.3 cm) strip of metal tab tape. Push a screw through a hole in the tape.

2 Screw it to the small block. Leave about ¼ inch (.6 cm) of the screw sticking out.

3 Push the metal tab tape to the side. Screw a screw into the wooden block. Leave about ¼ inch (.6 cm) of the screw sticking out.

continued on next page

MAKE THE POWER SOURCE

① Cut two 3½-inch (9 cm) strips of metal tab tape. Bend each strip in the middle. One half should stick up straight. Push a screw through a hole in one strip.

② Screw it to the end of the large block.

③ Push a screw through a hole in the second strip. Screw it to the large block 5 inches (12.7 cm) from the first strip.

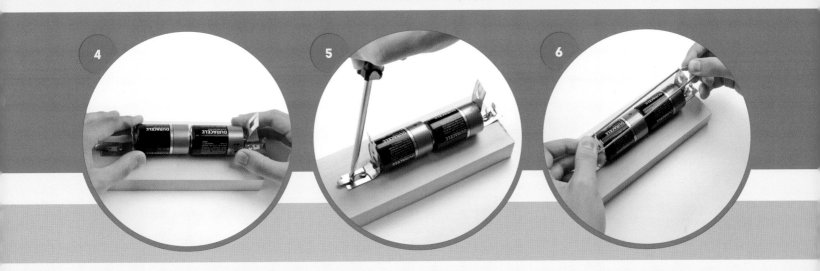

4 Put the **batteries** between the metal strips. Face them in the same direction.

5 Add a second screw to each of the strips on the large block. Leave about ¼ inch (.6 cm) of the screws sticking out.

6 Put a rubber band around the top of the metal strips.

continued on next page

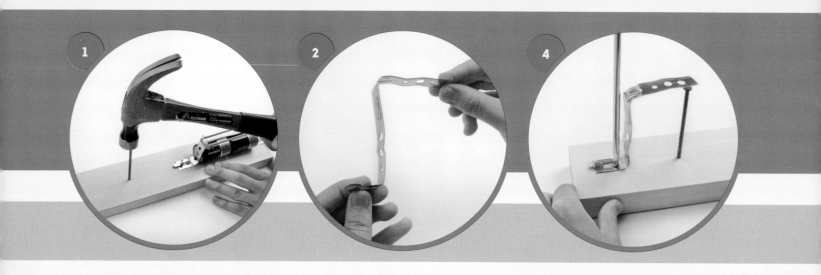

MAKE THE RECEIVER

① Hammer a nail into the large block. Put it 3 inches (7.5 cm) away from the **batteries**.

② Cut a 7-inch (17.8 cm) strip of metal tab tape. Bend one end 1 inch (2.5 cm). Bend the other end 3 inches (7.5 cm).

③ Push a screw through a hole in the short end of the strip.

④ Screw it to the long block about 2½ inches (6.3 cm) from the nail. The long end of the strip should cover the nail.

⑤ Cut two pieces of wire. Make one 10 inches (25 cm) long. Make the other 26 inches (66 cm) long. Strip 1 inch (2.5 cm) of coating off each end of the wires. (See page 19 for how to strip wire.)

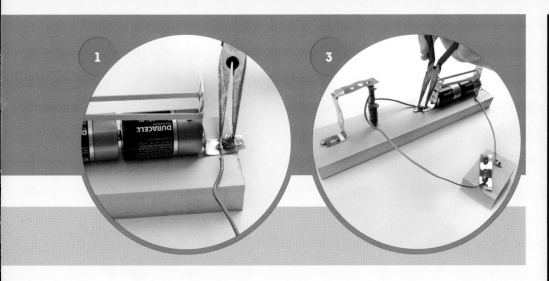

CONNECTING IT ALL

① Wrap one end of the short wire around the screw at the end of the receiver. Wrap the other end around a screw on the sender.

② Wrap one end of the long wire around the other screw on the sender.

③ Wrap about 12 inches (31 cm) of the long wire around the nail. Wrap the end around the other screw on the receiver.

④ Press the end of the sender down onto the nail. What happens?

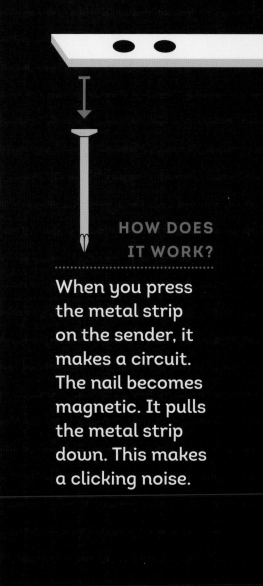

HOW DOES IT WORK?

When you press the metal strip on the sender, it makes a circuit. The nail becomes magnetic. It pulls the metal strip down. This makes a clicking noise.

MORSE CODE

Use your electric telegraph to send messages!

To send a dot, press the switch down. Let it go. To send a **dash**, hold it down three times longer. A space between letters is the same length as a dot. A space between words is the same length as a dash.

MORSE CODE

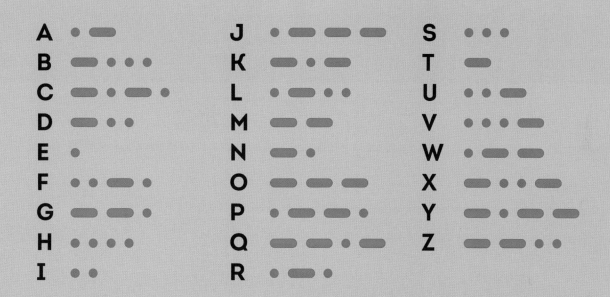

A	·—	J	·———	S	···
B	—···	K	—·—	T	—
C	—·—·	L	·—··	U	··—
D	—··	M	——	V	···—
E	·	N	—·	W	·——
F	··—·	O	———	X	—··—
G	——·	P	·——·	Y	—·——
H	····	Q	——·—	Z	——··
I	··	R	·—·		

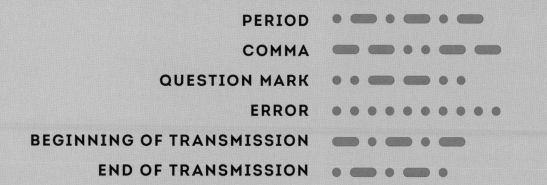

PERIOD	·—·—·—
COMMA	——··——
QUESTION MARK	··——··
ERROR	····································
BEGINNING OF TRANSMISSION	—·—·—
END OF TRANSMISSION	·—·—·

FLASH TELEGRAPH

Light up the night!

MATERIALS: 2 flashlights, 2 notepads, 2 pencils

CAN YOU
-.-. .- -.   -.-- --- ..-

READ THIS?
.-. . .- -..   - ....--..

HOW DOES IT WORK?

The US Navy still uses lights to send Morse code. They send messages from ship to ship. Light can be used to send dots and **dashes**. A short flash is like a dot. A long flash is like a dash.

USE MORSE CODE TO SEND MESSAGES

① Learn the Morse code alphabet on page 27.

② Write the message you want to send. **Translate** it into Morse code.

③ Use the flashlight to send the message to your friend. Use a short flash for a dot. Use a long flash for a dash.

④ Take turns sending Morse code messages. Write down the dots and dashes you get from your friend. Translate them to read the message.

CONCLUSION

The telegraph changed the world! It made sending and receiving messages a lot faster. The code invented for the telegraph is still in use. This book is the first step in discovering what's behind the telegraph. There is a lot more to find out.

Learn about improvements in communication. Look online or at the library. Think of telegraphy projects and experiments you can do on your own.

Put on your scientist thinking cap and go on a learning journey!

QUIZ

1. What was the key to distance messaging?

2. Morse code is still used today. **TRUE OR FALSE?**

3. Name one group that still uses flashlights in Morse code to send messages.

THINK ABOUT IT!

How did the telegraph change the world?

GLOSSARY

battery – a small container filled with chemicals that makes electrical power.

dash – a short, horizontal line used in punctuation or Morse code.

emergency – a sudden, unexpected, dangerous situation that requires immediate attention.

information – something known about an event or subject.

innovator – someone who does something in a new way.

material – something needed to make or build something else.

operator – someone whose job is to use a certain kind of machine.

relay – an electrically operated switch.

shuttle – a vehicle that takes people to and from a certain place or area.

translate – to change from one language or code into another.